Electromagnetism

CONTENTS

What Is Electricity?

When a blackout occurs, we realize how much we depend on electricity. Lights go out. Elevators, subway trains, computers, and many other important devices stop working. But what exactly is electricity?

Sometimes electricity is called **electric energy. Energy** is the ability to cause changes in matter or do work. Sound, light, and heat are other forms of energy. **Mechanical energy** is the energy of moving objects.

Energy can be changed from one form into another. A toaster changes electric energy into heat, or thermal, energy and light energy. Electric energy travels along wires inside the toaster. The wires give off thermal energy that toasts your bread. The wires also glow with light energy.

A telephone changes the sound energy of your voice into electric energy. After this energy travels along wires, the phone on the other end changes the electric energy back into sound energy. This lets a person hear your voice from across town or even from another country.

Electric energy results from the way electrons behave. **Electrons, protons,** and **neutrons** are the three main particles that make up atoms. All matter is made of **atoms.** Electrons move around the center, or **nucleus,** of an atom. Protons and neutrons make up the nucleus.

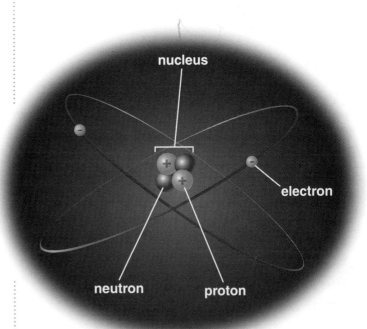

Electrons, protons, and neutrons are the three main types of particles inside an atom.

Electric charge is a basic property of matter. Protons have a positive electric charge. Electrons have a negative charge. Neutrons have a neutral charge. A material's overall charge can be positive, negative, or neutral.

Electric charges interact. Material with a negative electric charge will attract material with a positive charge. This is because unlike charges attract. Two materials with the same charge will repel, or push away from, each other. Like charges repel. **Electricity** is the interaction of electric charges. The interaction of charges at rest results in static electricity. The interaction of charges that are moving results in current electricity.

Static Electricity

Sometimes positive or negative charges build up on an object or material. This buildup of charge is called **static electricity.**

Rubbing objects together can cause static electricity. Electrons are transferred from one object to the other. For example, if you rub a balloon against your hair, electrons move from your hair to the balloon. Then the balloon has more electrons than protons. The balloon has a negative charge. Your hair is left with more protons than electrons. Your hair has a positive charge. The

Lightning is a giant discharge of static electricity. Lightning happens when negative charges in clouds jump to an area of positive charge on the ground.

charges on the balloon and your hair will pull toward each other because unlike charges attract. Your hair will stand up and stick to the balloon.

If enough charges build up on an object, they can discharge, or jump to an object with the opposite charge. You may even hear a small crackle or see a spark.

Current Electricity

Sparks are a discharge of static electricity, electrons jumping from place to place. But electrons also can flow steadily from place to place through some materials. This flow of electrons with their charge is called **current electricity,** or electric current.

Current electricity moves through some materials easily. These materials are called **conductors.** Many metals, such as copper and silver, are good conductors. Most wiring in a home is made of copper.

Current electricity does not flow well through certain materials. These materials are called **insulators.** Air, glass, rubber, and plastic are good insulators. The electric cord on a lamp is made with rubber or plastic as an insulator. A metal wire inside the rubber or plastic carries the current to the lamp. But the rubber or plastic on the outside keeps the current from flowing where it should not go.

Resistance is a measure of how well a material resists the flow of current electricity through it. Good conductors have low resistance. Good insulators have high resistance. The coils on a stove burner are made from a kind of metal that conducts but has a high resistance. When current moves through the coils, they become so hot that they glow.

Electric Circuits

Current can flow only when it has a complete path to follow. The path must return all the way to the place where it started. This path is called an **electric circuit.**

A flashlight has an electric circuit. The yellow line shows the complete path electric current follows.

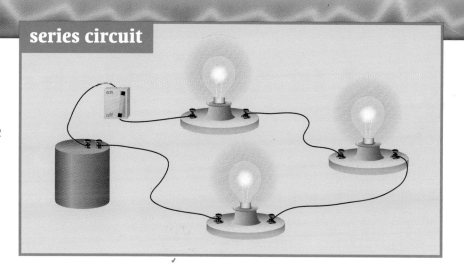

series circuit

All the bulbs in the circuit share the same path. If the switch were turned off, current would not flow to any of the bulbs.

A simple electric circuit has several parts. First, an electric circuit must have something to push electrons through the path. In a flashlight, one or more batteries supply energy to push the electrons.

Second, any object in the circuit must allow the current to flow through it. The flashlight bulb lights up when current flows through it.

Third, a conductor must connect the parts of the circuit. Wires are the conductors that connect the battery to the flashlight bulb.

Finally, a **switch** is used to open or close the circuit. When the circuit is closed, the path is complete. Current flows and the bulb lights. When the switch opens the circuit, the path is no longer complete. Current cannot flow and the bulb does not light.

Objects such as light bulbs or appliances can be connected to an electric circuit in one of two ways. In a **series circuit,** the objects are in a single path. In a series circuit of light bulbs, if you remove or turn off one bulb, the circuit opens. The current cannot flow, and none of the bulbs will light. In a **parallel circuit,** each object has its own path. Lights and appliances in homes are parts of parallel circuits. This lets you turn off the television while the lamp next to you stays on.

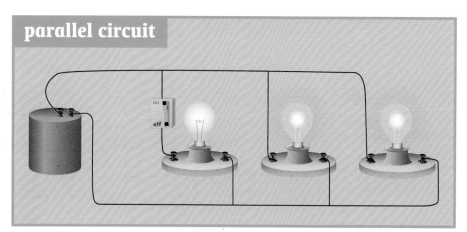

parallel circuit

Each bulb in the circuit has its own path. The switch to the first bulb is off, but current can still flow to the other two bulbs.

What Is Magnetism?

A **magnet** is a material that pulls, or attracts, the metals iron, cobalt, and nickel to it. The pull of a magnet on these materials is called magnetic force, or **magnetism.** Magnets also can attract other magnets and materials that contain iron, cobalt, or nickel. For example, steel contains iron, so it is attracted to a magnet.

Although magnets can be made in different sizes, shapes, and strengths, all magnets have the same properties. All magnets have two magnetic poles and a magnetic field. The **magnetic poles** are the places on a magnet where its magnetism is the strongest. The **magnetic field** is the space around a magnet where the magnet's force acts.

A bar magnet's poles are at its ends. Usually one pole of a bar magnet is labeled *N* and the other is labeled *S*. The *N* stands for north-seeking and the *S* stands for south-seeking. If you allow a bar magnet to hang freely from a string, the magnet will turn so that its north-seeking pole points north. Its south-seeking pole will point south.

Just as unlike electric charges attract each other, unlike magnetic poles attract each other. Like magnetic poles repel. So, an *N* pole and an *S* pole will pull toward each other. Two *N* poles will push away from each other.

A magnet's force does not act only at its poles. The magnetic field reaches in all directions around the magnet. Because a magnet's force acts at a distance from the magnet, a magnet can push or pull objects without touching them.

Even though we cannot see a magnetic field, we can see its effect. Iron filings sprinkled around a magnet form a pattern that shows the magnetic field. The filings gather along invisible lines called **field lines.** These lines show the direction and strength of the magnetic field. A magnet's force is stronger closer to the magnet and weaker farther away from the magnet.

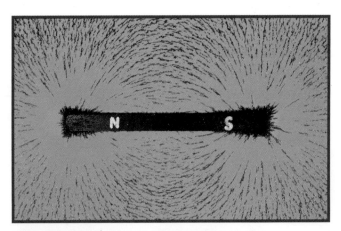

This pattern of iron filings shows the magnetic field of a bar magnet.

Some rocks are natural magnets. Lodestone, or magnetite, is a kind of natural magnet. Earth itself is like a giant bar magnet with magnetic north and south poles. Like other magnets, Earth is surrounded by a magnetic field. The needle of a compass is a small magnet that is attracted to Earth's north magnetic pole.

Magnets also can be made by people. When an iron or steel object is placed in a strong magnetic field, the object becomes a magnet. This happens because of the way atoms act. Each atom in an object has its own tiny magnetic field. The magnetic fields of the atoms in certain areas line up with one another. These areas are called **domains.** One object can have many domains. Each domain has an *N* pole and an *S* pole.

The domains in a piece of unmagnetized iron or steel point in different directions. But when the iron or steel is placed in a strong magnetic field, the domains in the object line up in the same direction. Their *N* poles point in one direction. Their *S* poles

Lodestone, a natural magnet, was found long ago in Magnesia, in Greece.

point in the other direction. The piece of iron or steel becomes a magnet.

Some metals are easy to turn into magnets, but their magnetism does not last. The domains in these metals do not stay lined up after the strong magnetic force is removed. These are **temporary magnets.** Stroking an iron or steel nail with a magnet will make a temporary magnet.

Other metals form **permanent magnets.** Their domains stay lined up, so their magnetism does not go away. Alnico is a mixture of the metals aluminum, nickel, and cobalt. Alnico is often used to manufacture permanent magnets.

When a material such as iron or steel is magnetized, its domains line up in the same direction.

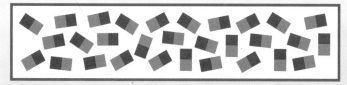

Domains before being magnetized

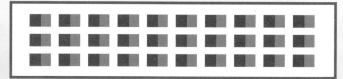

Domains after being magnetized

Using Electric Current to Make Magnets

In 1820 the Danish scientist Hans Christian Oersted made a discovery. He saw that an electric current flowing through a wire had an effect on a nearby compass. When the current was switched on and off, the compass needle moved. Oersted concluded that electric currents produce magnetic fields.

Oersted's discovery led to the invention of the electromagnet. A simple **electromagnet** can be made by wrapping a wire around an iron or steel object. When electric current flows through the wire, the object becomes a magnet. Electromagnets are temporary magnets. When the current is turned off, the magnetic field disappears and the iron or steel object is no longer a magnet.

Suppose we coil loops of wire around an iron nail and then connect both ends of the wire to a battery. Current flows through the wire, creating a magnetic field. The nail becomes a magnet. The nail will attract iron and steel objects. If we disconnect the wire from the battery, the nail will no longer attract iron or steel objects.

There are two ways to make the magnetic field of an electromagnet stronger. One way is to wrap more loops of wire around the iron or steel object. The other way is to increase the amount of current flowing through the wire.

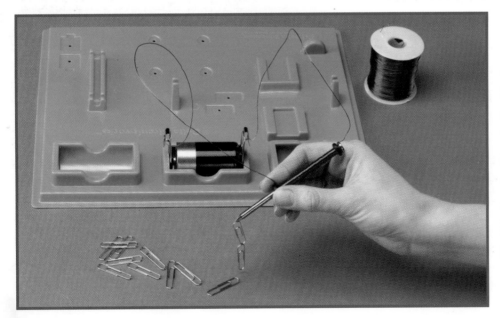

A simple electromagnet uses both electric and magnetic forces. This electromagnet can be made stronger by wrapping more loops of wire around the iron nail or by adding more batteries.

Large electromagnets can be used to pick up and sort metal at a recycling center.

electromagnet. The electromagnet causes a metal disk to vibrate. This produces energy in the form of sound waves. We hear those sound waves as a person's voice.

Electromagnets are useful because their magnetism can be turned on and off. Some machines have very strong electromagnets. Machines of this kind can pick up old cars and move them to a crushing machine in a scrapyard. They also can move huge steel beams at building sites.

Many everyday devices use smaller electromagnets. Doorbells, telephones, and automatic doors are just a few examples. In a telephone, electric signals from the phone line enter the earpiece and pass through an

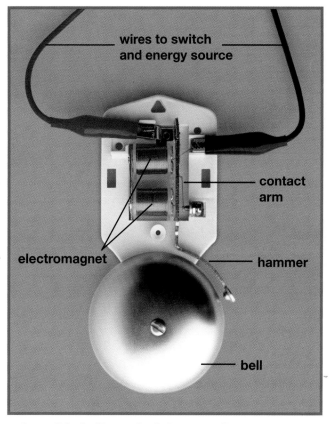

wires to switch and energy source

contact arm

electromagnet

hammer

bell

When this bell's switch is turned on, current flows through wires to an electromagnet. The electromagnet attracts a metal contact arm. The contact arm moves a hammer that strikes the bell.

Using Magnets to Make Electric Current

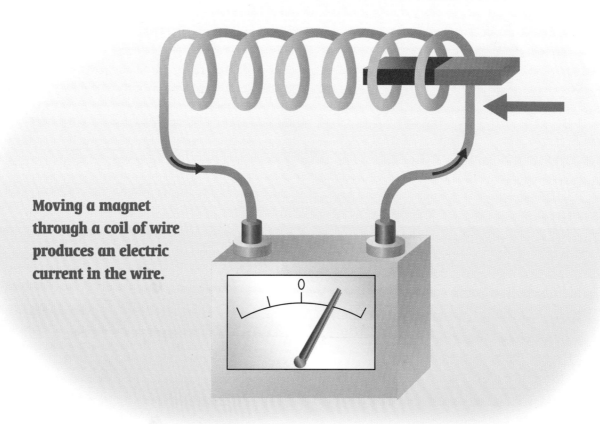

Moving a magnet through a coil of wire produces an electric current in the wire.

Oersted discovered that electric currents produce magnetic fields. Other scientists wondered if a magnetic field could be used to produce an electric current. Two scientists who studied this question were Michael Faraday of England and Joseph Henry of the United States.

Around 1831 both Faraday and Henry did the same kind of experiment. They moved a magnet through a coil of wire. They saw that an electric current could be produced in the wire as long as either the coil or the magnet was moving.

Moving the coil or magnet changes the amount of magnetic field affecting the coil. This occurs because a magnetic field acts in all directions around a magnet and is stronger at the poles than in other places. The change in the amount of magnetic field affecting the coil produces the electric current. If the magnetic field is not changing, current does not flow in the coil.

Generators

A **generator** is a machine that uses changing magnetic fields to produce electric current. Generators make it possible for homes and businesses to have electricity. One type of generator moves magnets past coils of wire. Another type of generator makes a wire coil turn within a magnet's field. As long as the wire coil turns or the magnets move, the amount of magnetic field affecting the coil changes, and current flows through the coil.

In most power plants, turbines are used to turn the coils or magnets in a generator. A turbine is a wheel attached to a rod. As the wheel turns, the rod also turns. The rod spins the coils or magnets inside the generator, making current flow through the coils.

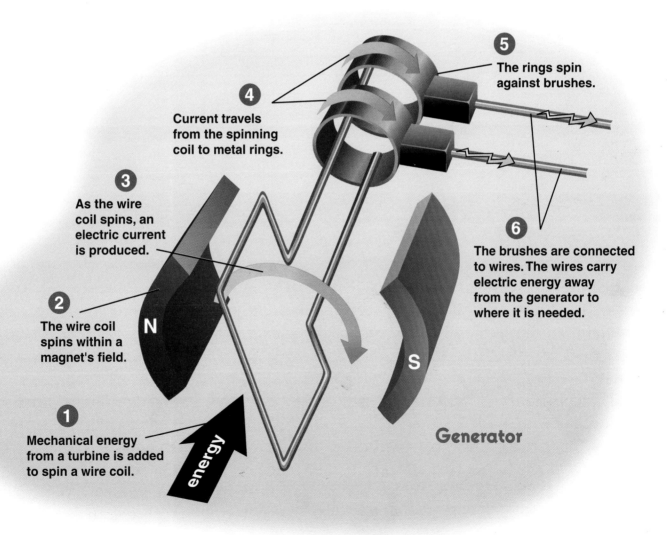

5 The rings spin against brushes.

4 Current travels from the spinning coil to metal rings.

3 As the wire coil spins, an electric current is produced.

2 The wire coil spins within a magnet's field.

N

6 The brushes are connected to wires. The wires carry electric energy away from the generator to where it is needed.

S

1 Mechanical energy from a turbine is added to spin a wire coil.

energy

Generator

A generator does not create energy. Instead, it changes mechanical energy into electric energy. Turbines need some kind of mechanical energy to make them turn. In most power plants, turbines are turned by steam. Water is changed to steam using heat produced by burning fuels such as coal, oil, or natural gas. The steam hits large blades on the turbine, making the turbine spin. In a few places, thermal energy from the sun is used to produce steam to turn a turbine. Rows of mirrors collect and focus sunlight to change water into steam.

Wind and moving water are other sources of mechanical energy for a turbine. Water that comes from a dam can spin a turbine. Dams are built on rivers to hold back water in reservoirs. When gates on a dam open, water flows down through a large pipe. The water hits the turbine and makes it spin.

Electric power plants are often built at large dams. The mechanical energy of flowing water is used to turn turbines in huge generators to create electric energy.

How Do Electric Motors Work?

A generator changes mechanical energy into electric energy. An **electric motor** works in the opposite way. A motor uses electric energy to produce mechanical energy, the energy of a moving object. This motion can be used to do work.

Electric motors are all around us. A motor moves the blades of a blender that makes a milkshake. Power tools like saws and drills have motors. Washers and dryers have motors.

A simple electric motor has three parts. The first part is a permanent magnet. The magnet is fixed in one place and cannot move. The second part is a temporary magnet. This is an electromagnetic coil that rotates between the poles of the fixed magnet. The third part is a device that changes the direction of the current flowing through the electromagnetic coil.

Each pole of the motor's electromagnetic coil is attracted to the opposite pole of the fixed magnet. When current passes through the

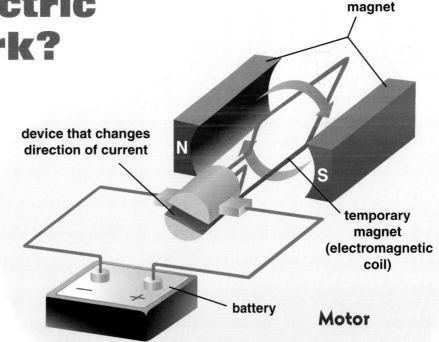

permanent magnet

device that changes direction of current

N

S

temporary magnet (electromagnetic coil)

battery

Motor

The electricity for an electric motor can come from a battery or from household current.

electromagnetic coil, it turns so that the unlike poles on the two magnets line up. Just as the poles line up, the direction of current reverses in the electromagnetic coil. This reverses the poles of the electromagnetic coil. Now two like poles are near each other. The electromagnetic coil turns again so the unlike poles will line up. As the direction of the current keeps changing, the coil keeps spinning. This motion is used to do work, such as turning the blades of a fan.

Samuel F. B. Morse (1791–1872)

Samuel Morse was born in Charlestown, Massachusetts. He studied art and science at Yale University.

On a trip home from Europe, Morse heard people talking about electromagnets. Morse had an idea. What if electrical signals could be used to send messages across long distances? At that time, writing letters was the best way of communicating over long distances.

A telegraph is a device that uses electromagnets to send signals along wires. The first telegraph was built in Switzerland in 1774, but it used many wires and was not very practical. Morse completed a working model of the first single-wire telegraph in 1837. But not until 1844 did he make a telegraph system that could be put into use.

With money from the United States government, Morse built a telegraph line that could send messages between Baltimore, Maryland, and Washington, D.C. Within ten years, 54,000 kilometers (34,000 miles) of telegraph wires crisscrossed the United States.

Morse and his partner, Alfred Vail, also invented a signaling code, called Morse code. The code uses dots and dashes to represent letters and numbers. The "dot" is sent as a short pulse of electric current. The "dash" is sent as a longer burst of electric current. Using Morse code, messages could be sent across wires to a receiver. The receiver printed the dots and dashes on a strip of paper moving beneath a pen.

Samuel Morse's telegraph was the first invention that let people send messages instantly over long distances.

The Morse code is printed on the inside back cover of this book.

About the Uses of Electromagnets

Many everyday devices use small electromagnets, from doorbells and telephones to toasters, earphones, and CD players. Electromagnets are also part of the electric motors inside hair dryers, refrigerators, and kitchen blenders. Even some cars are powered by electric motors.

Electromagnets are also used in hospitals. An MRI machine uses a huge, powerful electromagnet to take pictures of the inside of the human body. Doctors can study the pictures that are made by the MRI machine.

Someday you might take a ride on a train that is moved by electromagnets. A maglev train uses the forces of magnets to rise above a guideway. *Maglev* stands for *magnetic levitation*. Because the train does not touch the guideway, there is no friction from a track to slow it down. Maglev trains can reach speeds greater than 500 kilometers (about 300 miles) per hour!

Electromagnets have many surprising uses.

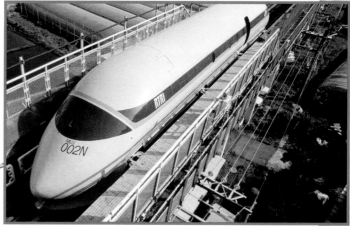

One type of maglev train has electromagnets under the train and on the guideway. The like poles of the electromagnets repel each other, pushing the train up.

Glossary

atom smallest unit of a substance that still has all the properties of that substance

conductor material through which electric current passes easily

current electricity electric charges that can flow steadily through a material; also called *electric current*

domain group of atoms whose magnetic fields are lined up with one another

electric charge basic property of matter that can be positive or negative and that changes when matter gains or loses electrons

electric circuit closed path along which electric current flows

electric energy form of energy that results from the way electrons behave

electricity interaction of electric charges; can be static (at rest) or current (flowing)

electric motor device that uses magnets to change electric energy into mechanical energy

electromagnet temporary magnet made when electric current flows through a wire wrapped around an iron or steel core

electron tiny particle that moves around the nucleus of an atom; an electron has a negative electric charge

energy ability to cause changes in matter or do work

field lines invisible lines around a magnet that show the direction and strength of the magnetic field; also called *lines of force*

generator device that uses magnets to change mechanical energy into electric energy

insulator material through which electric current does not easily pass

magnet material that has a magnetic field around it and so attracts metals containing iron, cobalt, or nickel

magnetic field space around a magnet where the force of the magnet acts

magnetic poles places on a magnet where the magnetic force is the strongest

magnetism force of a magnet that attracts the metals iron, cobalt, and nickel and materials that contain these metals

mechanical energy form of energy produced by a moving object

neutron tiny particle that is part of the nucleus of an atom; a neutron has no electric charge

nucleus center of an atom

parallel circuit circuit that connects two or more objects so that the current flows along a different path to each object

permanent magnet magnet that holds its magnetic properties for a long time

proton tiny particle that is part of the nucleus of an atom; a proton has a positive electric charge

resistance measure of how well a material resists the flow of current through it

series circuit circuit that connects two or more objects, one after the other, so that the current flows in a single path to all objects

static electricity electric charges at rest that can build up on a material and discharge, or jump from one material to another, but do not flow steadily

switch device used to start and stop the flow of electric current in a circuit

temporary magnet magnet that loses its magnetism after a short time